T0194705

The
CRIMINAL INJUSTICE SYSTEM

The CRIMINAL INJUSTICE SYSTEM

A True Story

CAROL SPENCER and TERRY LOWERY

THE CRIMINAL INJUSTICE SYSTEM
A TRUE STORY

iUniverse books may be ordered through booksellers or by contacting:

iUniverse
1663 Liberty Drive
Bloomington, IN 47403
www.iuniverse.com
1-800-Authors (1-800-288-4677)

ISBN: 978-1-5320-8099-9 (sc)
ISBN: 978-1-5320-8100-2 (e)

Print information available on the last page.

iUniverse rev. date: 08/28/2019

ACKNOWLEDGEMENTS

First of all I want to thank God for urging me to write to Terry, if that had not happened there would be no story. Next I want to thank my good friend Linda Morgan for going to the prison that first time with me, and then taking me to her late brother, Atty. Joseph Grolimund, who told me what to do, and called the prison to make sure there were no slip ups, so that they did not go ahead with the execution.

I also want to thank my good friends Jan and Martin Reef who stood by both Terry and I while he was in prison, and when he got out. They were a comfort, and encouragement to both of us, and still are. Martin even went to some of the clemency hearings on Terry's behalf.

We are also grateful for Pastors Tim and Dawn Brown who came to our house and greeted Terry when he was brought home, and took a video of that precious time because I had to work.

Last, but by no means least, I want to thank my friend, Dr. Carol Goodbar-Brook, who encouraged me to continue writing the book, looked it over and made suggestions. Without her belief that we had a story to tell, this book may never have been written.

PREFACE

et me introduce myself. I do not consider myself as an author, unless you would count the thousands of progress notes I have written over my 40+ years of experience in the field of social work and mental health psychotherapy. I am a simple person, perhaps in more ways than one. I grew up in a small town in Ohio, went to Ohio University, married my high school sweetheart, and had the then typical 2 children. I made sure that they were two or more years apart so that each one would have time to be the baby. I tried to do everything right. I always went to church, and cannot remember a time when I was not an authentic believer in God, and Jesus Christ. However, life, fate, God, time or whatever you want to call it, has a way of changing us, whether we want it to or not. I had a good life, and I still do, but I did not expect or plan for it to change like it did from just reading a simple newspaper article.

I have always had a lot of empathy for the plight of other people, as you might expect or hope to find in someone who is a social worker/ counselor. I guess that is why that newspaper article got to me. Also, at that time my children were grown, my marriage was stagnant, and I still had not yet fulfilled my own career dreams of getting my master's degree in social work. That is when God really spoke to me, and sent me on the path of this story, and my life has never been the same since. It was Terry who encouraged me to go back to college and get my master's degree, so I owe as much to him as he does to me.

CHAPTER 1

The Criminal Injustice System

There I was 23 years old, and standing in front of a judge, and a courtroom full of people. I knew what he was going to say before he said it. I knew I wouldn't live to see 30. I had always known that. My mind was racing. My heart was beating faster than it ever had before. I had to be strong. I couldn't let them see me sweat, or even worse, cry. I wouldn't let the bastards see that they had gotten to me. The verdict came down hard, DEATH IN THE ELECTRIC CHAIR! My heart sank, and my knees started to buckle. NO, I told myself. Don't react like they expect you to. Be a man. Be strong. Reporters started to swarm around me. I told them, trying to be as bad as they were, 'That chair is not going to get me. I am going to get right up out of that chair'.

Almost 10 years later, I did just that. By the grace of God, I was given a good lawyer, Atty. Judith Menadue. She and some others got me off of Death Row, or X-Row, as they called it in there. The Fort Wayne Herald quoted me when that happened saying I was right. That was the only time they said that I was right. From the time when I first got arrested to the present day the press and the public have done nothing but convict, defame, and mistreat me just like my grandparents did when I was a child. They made me out to be some kind of a demonic person way before the judge read the verdict.

The media helped to convince the public that I was guilty, when there was no real evidence that I committed the crime, except for a forced confession which the police got after a grueling interrogation in which they kept me in a room and made me go without food, water, sleep, and warmth for a couple of days. Also, they injected me with a drug, and when I resisted, they injected me anyway. I couldn't call anyone, because I had no one to call, and even if had someone to call, they would not let me call. They kept shouting at me, "Tell us what we want to hear. Tell us what we want to hear". Finally, to get them off my back I told them what they wanted to hear, which was the biggest lie I ever told, and the worst one. Years later, I told my wife the name of the drug they injected in me, and when she looked it up in the PDR she found that if a person was not psychotic when they took the drug, it made them, psychotic.

In my 26 years in prison I learned more about the criminal injustice system than I ever really wanted to know. It is amazing how well it all works together to keep the poor, and disenfranchised people down and prevent them from getting the same kind of justice that the knowledgeable and/or wealthy people are able to get. A person does not have to be black to be mistreated by the justice system. All they have to be is poor, lower middle class, and have no money or support system. The criminal injustice system is all about money and power, just like the prisons are. If one can hire a good lawyer, or pay off a guard in prison, they can get almost anything that a person can get outside of prison. If one hires the wrong lawyer, they just waste their money.

A major problem is, how does a person in prison know who is a good lawyer, and how do they get in touch with one if they have no one on the outside who will help them? Even if they find a lawyer, how do they know if that lawyer will really be on their side? Also, if their case goes to court, they still have to depend on the opinions and biases of the judge, jury, prosecutor, and again the press and media. The bottom line is, how guilty a person looks, even if they are not guilty at all.

In my case the other defendant was a juvenile, and at that time a juvenile could not be sent to prison, or given a death sentence. Since I was over 18, had no money, no family support, no paid lawyer, and no positive influence, I was a prime target for the injustice system to work perfectly.

My childhood was one I would like to forget. As a child I suffered severe physical, mental, emotional, and sexual abuse. I spent days at a time locked in a closet, with no bathroom, food, or light. I had cigarettes put out on my arms. Once I spilled some paint, and I got burned for that. My first sexual contacts were with my grandma, grandpa, and older brother. My grandma would put me over her knees and use her fingers and other objects and insert them into my anus. She gave me baths every day, and told me to show her that I loved her by making me perform oral sex on her. My brother, and I were made to have sex with each other while they both watched. My biological mother and her sister had suffered the same kind of treatment, but my mother thought that since we were boys, it wouldn't happen to us. She gave me to my grandparents when I was only two years old because her husband did not like kids. My mother and aunt knew what was going on, and they did nothing to stop it.

There was no one for me to tell because I was led to believe that no one would believe me. I carried this with me all my life, and the only way I knew of dealing with it as a child, and young adult was by using drugs and alcohol to numb the pain.

My grandpa made bootleg liquor, so I was allowed to start drinking when I was only 7 or 8 years of age. Between the beatings and the sexual abuse, the alcohol helped to dull the emotional pain.

At times when my grandma thought we were getting out of hand, she would put a shotgun to her head, and tell us she was going to blow her brains out, if we didn't stop what we were doing. When my grandpa got drunk, he would shoot at us. He would tell us to take out the garbage, and when we would, that was when he would use us for target practice. Later on when I told my wife that story, she said, "Terry, What did you do when he shot at you?" I told her I stopped taking out the garbage.

My grandma used to take care of elderly people in our home. When I was about 8 years old, I saw her sit and do nothing while one poor old woman choked on a piece of food. I pleaded with her to do something, but she just let the poor woman die right there in front of us. I felt sick, and wanted to throw up.

Our house was very violent. Every night my brother and I were made to sleep with either my grandma or grandpa. Grandma would always say, "Show me you love me". Then I was forced to give her oral sex, and she would put things inside of me. Grandpa would make me give him oral sex, and then he would sodomize me. During my childhood I was told that sex was love and love was sex.

We moved around a lot during my childhood, and we usually ended up moving to the country so we could be away from everyone. Anytime that someone would start to ask questions, we would move. My only freedom from it all happened when my grandma died back in 1974. Then I was left with my grandpa who continued to beat me and rape me.

One time after a beating, I robbed him and ran away. They took me to court, and I told the judge about the beatings, and told him I did not want to go back home. The judge said that they would have to find a place for me, and sent me home that night. That night my grandpa nearly killed me. A few nights later I robbed my grandpa at knifepoint, and ran away again. A few days later I was caught and sent to jail. To me that was better than being sent back to my grandpa. The judge asked me, "Why couldn't you wait?" I told him, but he sent me to Richmond State Hospital for drug treatment, and from there he sent me to Whites Institute, which is a juvenile residential treatment center. The court system never worked that well for me. Why didn't they send my grandparents to jail for child abuse? Why didn't someone report them to Child Protective Services?

After my time at Whites Institute the only person who would take me was my aunt, my mother's sister. She was not much better than my grandparents. She would put the "make" on me, and bring anyone to be with me, both male and female. I learned to shut down all my feelings until I forgot how to feel altogether. I didn't care if I lived or died. Many nights I would wish that I would never wake up because I thought that there was no help or hope for me. I went from one bad relationship to another. The only time I was happy was when I was playing music. I learned to play drums and guitar. By playing music, I could lose myself, and forget about what was going on around me.

I was in prison for 26 years for a murder I did not commit, and the court system did not work for me. I tried everything within my power to prove my innocence, and every effort was blocked, hindered, and/or sidetracked by some legal glitch. The court system in Fort Wayne and the Department of Corrections in Indiana should be looked into. All the charges against me were dropped during a Post-Conviction Release hearing because there was no proof except circumstantial evidence, and a forced confession to connect me to the murder. DNA evidence was not known back then, and when we tried to have it done later on the evidence at the crime scene, it was denied by the court.

My death sentence was overturned in 1994, and yet they would not release me from prison. The only way I got out of prison was by rehabilitating myself, and taking advantage of every program that had a time cut connected to it. Fortunately, the prison where I last was had a program that offered college courses from two credited Indiana colleges, Ball State University and Grace College. I chose Grace College because I became a Christian while in prison, and wanted to get a Christian education. I was blessed with a bachelor's degree in business, with a minor in Biblical Studies. The prison stopped providing those resources about a year after I was released from prison. With the way that my life had been, it was hard for me to believe that I was able to get a college degree. That degree has really helped restore some hope that I never had while I was growing up.

With the help of my wife, who wrote up lengthy papers describing all of the things I had accomplished while in prison, I applied for Clemency at least 4 times. Each time when we went before the Parole Board, or Clemency Board, which was the same thing, they would ask the same questions. They would ask me what happened, and why I thought I should be released. They would also ask me what I had done to better myself, even though they had it all written out and handed to them. Several times, I had other people vouch for my credibility, such as ministers, and friends of my wife, who had also become my friends. No matter how much I had done, and no matter how good my record was, the request for an early release was never even considered. At that time we learned that within an 18 or 19 year period, only 3 people had ever been granted Clemency. One was released because he was dying, and the reason for the other two was unknown. In the last years that I applied for Clemency the applications got conveniently lost inside of the prison. Eventually, I gave up filing for it and the injustice system won again.

The only good thing that came out of all of this is that while on Death Row I met and married the love of my life, Carol. She stood by me all the time when not one person in my family ever did. She helped me get through a lot of pain, and helped me learn how to feel again. She taught me what, "true love" really is.

CHAPTER 2

I was just an ordinary housewife that day who was leisurely reading the newspaper when I came across this newspaper article that was entitled, "They Just Want to Watch Me Burn". That title caught my attention. It was written by an inmate on Death Row. He had tried to commit suicide by taking a razor apart, and slitting his jugular vein. When the blood started dripping down on the fellow in the lower bunk, the guards were summoned, and the man in the article was taken to the prison hospital where they gave him transfusions which saved his life. (He later told me that he heard that he only had about two pints of blood still left in his body when they got him to the hospital.)The man in the article was angry because they saved his life because in his warped way of thinking, at that time, they only saved his life for one reason, and that reason was so they could watch him die in the electric chair, rather than die the way he wanted to. At that time, he thought that the justice system, and the whole world was comprised of mean and hateful people who were sadistic, mean, uncaring, and despicable, like his grandparents and the correctional people had been. He thought that all of the public wanted to shame and humiliate him more than they had already done, and that is why they saved his life, and that made him angry.

As I read the article a feeling of deep sadness came over me because I felt that this was an individual who had never been loved, and did not know that there were more good people in this world than bad ones. My heart went out to him. As I read the article I thought to myself that he needed to know that there were good people in this world. Then I put down the newspaper, said to myself, that this is not my problem, and went about doing my household chores. I thought the person in the article must be a really bad and callous person, but something told me that was not true.

Then suddenly, something strange happened. A little voice inside of me said, *"Write to him"*. I immediately responded with a vehement, NO, I can't do that. Why would I write to a man in prison? After a couple of minutes arguing with myself, I heard it again. *"Write to Him"*. Once more I kept finding reasons why I should not write to him, saying, I am married, I can't help him, or do anything for him, and kept cleaning my house. Then the little voice spoke again, only this time it was more urgent, and insistent. It said, **"Write to him, Write to him, WRITE TO HIM"!** When that happened I knew I was not hallucinating, and was starting to recognize where this little voice and idea was coming from.

No amount of my feeble reasoning could quiet the voice which I now positively identified as God's Holy Spirit because the urgency just kept increasing, and it did not come at long intervals anymore, but kept repeatedly telling me to write to him. I reasoned that it could not be the devil because the devil never tells us to do something good for someone. Finally, I said, Ok, Lord, I will write to him, but you have to tell me what to say. I am not one to argue with the Lord very long because He had never spoken so urgently and clearly as He did that day. So, I got a pen and paper, and went into my prayer room, sat down on the floor by my coffee table, and started to write, listening to what the Lord told me to write. I don't remember exactly what I said that day, but the essence of it went something like this:

Dear Terry,

I read your article in the newspaper, and I wanted to let you know that there are a lot of good people who do care about other people out here. I believe that God wanted me to write to you to tell you that He loves you, and no matter what you have done, you can be forgiven. In the Bible there is a story about a man named, Saul, who God later named, Paul. Saul went about persecuting Christians, and even approved while one man, Steven, was stoned to death. No matter how bad Saul/Paul was, Jesus saw great value in him, and when Saul was on his way to Damascus to persecute more Christians, Jesus appeared to him, knocked him off of his horse, and blinded him. Later Jesus appeared to another Christian, and had him pray for Saul and when Saul received his sight, he got his name changed to Paul, and he went on to be the first missionary, and wrote much of the New Testament.

If God can do that for Paul, He can do that for you too. We are all sinners, and it is only because Jesus paid the price for our sins that by believing in Him, we are forgiven, and can have eternal life. Read John 3:16, and you will see what I am talking about. You have tried everything else, what do you have to lose by giving God a chance?

God Bless you,

Carol

That was the essence of what I wrote that day. After I wrote that letter, which I truly know that God told me to write, I sealed it, and sent it. Then, I sarcastically, said to God, I did what you told me to do, so now leave me alone about this. With that done, I tore up the newspaper article, and thought I had washed my hands of the whole situation. (Little did I know how that one step of obedience would change my life.)

About a week later I got a letter in the mail that was stamped that it was from a prison. When I received it, I said, 'Oh No', before I opened it. Much to my surprise, inside the envelope was one of the sweetest and most unexpected kind letter. That letter did not sound at all like the one in the newspaper that I had read that day. Instead the writer was very humble, and polite. He said:

Dear Carol,

I got your letter, and I want to thank you for writing to me. It is not too many people who will write to someone on Death Row I

hope that it doesn't embarrass you to have a
letter stamped from a prison coming to your
house. I read the scripture you told me about,
and they made a lot of sense, so I got out my
Bible, and have been reading it ever since.
Thank you again, and God Bless you too.

Terry Lowery

When I received that letter from Terry, I cannot describe how good it made me feel. At that time in my life I was not feeling too good about myself. I felt that no one listened to me, or paid any attention to anything I had to say, much less believe me enough to pick up a Bible and start reading it. My two children had recently left home, and my husband was an alcoholic who did not hear a word I said, and cared less if I said anything at all. He would laugh if I mentioned anything spiritual, or about God. Therefore, when a person who I thought was a hardened criminal, listened to me, and actually started reading the Bible because of a simple letter I had written him. I was amazed and dumbfounded to learn what God had done with just a little reluctant effort on my part.

That one little step of obedience to the voice of God which took place back in 1986, has changed my life forever in more ways than I could have ever imagined at that time in my life, and set my feet on a very different course.

With the knowledge and approval of my first husband, I continued to write to Terry. I would send him scriptures and words of encouragement to help him endure his life on Death Row. In turn, he drew pictures which he sent to me, and told me about his life. He also encouraged me to pursue my dream of going to graduate school, and getting my master's degree in social work.

In one letter he asked me to come up and visit him at the prison. He said that his family had disowned him, and had never been there for him even when he was a child. I thought about his request, and convinced my good friend, Linda, to go with me to the prison to meet him. We set aside a time and we drove 100 miles up to the prison in Michigan City, Indiana, where they kept the Death Row inmates.

The day that Linda and I drove up to the prison we were both scared, leery, and somewhat giddy about going into a prison for the first time, and meeting someone we did not know. We had to give our names at the front desk, lock all of our belongings in a locker, take all of our jewelry off, and then get frisked before going through those first barred doors. Then they took us into a little room that was like a cage, with bars on two sides, and brick walls on the other sides. Terry was already sitting at a table. We introduced ourselves, and sat down. Terry was excited to have visitors because he had not seen anyone from the outside for several months. He talked very fast, and we all found a lot to talk about.

At one point Terry turned to me and said, "Carol, I have given up my appeal. Do you think I should try to reinstate it?" I was shocked by the question, and quickly replied, Terry, of course you should reinstate it. Where there is life, there's hope. He then said,

"I have been trying to get hold of my court appointed lawyer, but he won't accept my calls, and I don't know how to get my case reinstated. It was at that point that my friend, Linda, spoke up. She said, "What you need is a good lawyer ".Terry replied, "How can I get a good lawyer, I have no money, and my public defender won't take my calls." Linda then said, "My brother is a lawyer, and after we leave here today, we will go over to Elkhart, and pay him a visit", and that is what we did.

Linda's brother had his law office in his home, and walking into his office was an experience of its own. There were papers stacked everywhere, and only a single pathway through them to get to where we could sit down. Nevertheless, he was friendly, and glad to see his sister. Linda told me that he often took cases for people who had no money to pay lawyers pro bono.

Her brother, Joe, asked me if I knew anyone who had any influence, or was in any high office. I told him I had served on a church committee with a man who had once been the head of the state police, and was now the temporary Dept. of Correction Commissioner. He said that I should contact him, to get Terry's appeal reinstated.

Terry was scheduled to be executed in June of 1986 if he did not get his appeal reinstated. It was about March or April of that year when Linda and I first visited Terry, and then talked to her brother. I immediately called the D.O.C. Commissioners office and asked to speak to the commissioner, but he was on vacation. When I told the office manager what I needed to talk to him about, she directed my call to one of the lawyers in that office. When I explained the situation to the lawyer, he said, "That's not right that his public defender won't take his calls." Then he said, "I'll take care of it, and re-instate Terry's appeal, and call the execution off", and he did it. I did not get that man's name, but he did what he said he would do, and the appeal was re-instated and the execution was called off.

I kept calling the prison to make sure they got the message about the execution being called off, and so did Linda's brother. We wanted to make sure that there was not going to be any slip ups. The prison did not notify Terry until 3 days before he was scheduled to be executed. When the guard came to notify

Terry, he was in the shower. When he heard the news that the execution was called off he later told me that he dropped down on his knees, and praised the Lord. The man who once tried to take his own life, was now praising God for saving his life.

Later on Terry told me that was not the only time his life had been saved. When he was born, He had a twin brother, and his mother fell down a flight of stairs when she was 8 or 9 months pregnant, and his twin brother was killed by that accident.

Also, when he was 9 or 10 years old, and was living out in the country, Terry was watching a farmer as he was harvesting his crops, and he didn't hear, and/or pay attention to traffic on the road in front of his house, and as he was crossing the road he got hit by a pick-up truck. The back wheel missed his head by inches, and one of his front teeth got knocked out.

CHAPTER 3

When I was first getting to know Terry we had a lot of lengthy conversations, and he told me that he did not commit the crime that he was serving time for, and that the crime was really committed by the 15 year old boy who got off easy by going to Boys School. While it is generally believed that one cannot trust anything that someone in prison says, I was not like that because I had worked with a lot of different people, and found many honest people among them who, for one reason or another, had been not believed, not given a chance, or disenfranchised. My philosophy has always been to give a person the benefit of the doubt, and the Bible tells us that we are not to judge other people. Also, there was something about Terry that caused me to believe that he was not capable of committing the crime he was accused of because he has a gentle and loving spirit.

However, to be on the safe side, I thought I would do some investigating of his situation myself, so I went up to the public library in Fort Wayne and researched the newspaper articles that were published at the time of the crime, and for several years before the crime happened. I learned that there had been a period of 7 to 10 years prior to the murder where the Fort Wayne police department had not solved many violent crimes, and the public was angry, and wanted someone to get caught and punished. On October 15, 1985, there was an article in the Fort Wayne Journal Gazette that talked about the large number of homicides and violent crimes in Allen County, Indiana that year. The officials said they were alarmed because the record was 25 homicides in 1971, and 1981. Here are some of the articles from the Fort Wayne Journal Gazette which were written at the time of the trial.

> "Total number of Allen county homicides reported to police this year is 23. Some killings appear to have been committed in a frenzy. Others appear to have been committed executions- style, carried out in the most cold-blooded fashion one could imagine. Officials say they're not alarmed by the numbers of homicides in this community this year. The record here is 25, established in 1976 and 1981. Officials also note that other cities the size of Fort Wayne have many more killings, which is true."

Another article written a month later in the same Fort Wayne newspaper on November 9,1985 said:

> "The shooting deaths early Thursday of Martin, 'Gene' Rubrake and Theodore Bosler, of West Wayne Street bring the number of homicides to 27 for Allen County. That breaks the record of 25 set in 1976 & 1981"

There were several other articles written in the Journal Gazette at that time which were about Terry, the death penalty, and about the electric chair, which was the method of corporal punishment used in that period of time. Terry's trial took place in December of 1985. Two of the articles for and against capital punishment showed pictures of the electric chair, and went into detail about how it killed the person. One article even illustrated how a man was strapped into it while being executed. Another article called it, "Old Sparky". The negative press prior to and concurrent with Terry's trial, and the mention of all of the unsolved murders and violent crimes in the city during the 10 years prior to the murder escalated the public's cry for something to be done, and someone to be caught and punished.

The public wanted revenge, and Terry happened to be a good candidate for that revenge. He had all the qualifications.

He had been rejected by his parents, given to his grandparents who abused him, he had a history of drug abuse, and a juvenile record, (which is not supposed to be counted against a person as an adult). In addition, his wife, at that time, testified against him, and he had no support system.

Since Terry had been victimized since he was 2 years old, he had developed what is known as 'victim behavior'. That describes behavior of a person who has been put down and discriminated against so much that they are easily convinced that they will get blamed anyway, so they just give up and admit guilt when it is not true, or they agree to take the blame for someone else. One common example is a person who flinches when someone close to them raises their hand because they think someone is going to hit them. Chronically depressed people often succumb to victim behavior because they feel they are beyond hope, and unworthy of receiving anything good in life. That is the kind of condition Terry was in at that time in his life, and the legal system in Fort Wayne could sense it. The officials in Fort Wayne had to solve a crime, and Terry was the answer to their problem.

Through the many years of knowing Terry as well as working with other disadvantaged people I have learned a lot about the legal system, I have found some major things to be true.

- It is more difficult to prove that someone is innocent than it is to prove them guilty.
- It is more difficult to get the courts to believe the truth than it is for them to believe a lie.
- It is extremely difficult to get justice if one does not have some type of influence, money, or a good lawyer.

  Also, a common person does not know how to select a good lawyer, and no one can tell

whether the lawyer one does obtain will really
be on their side.

You may ask, how do I know that the above is true? I know
it is true because I have lived through it, along with Terry. I
had one female prosecutor from Fort Wayne tell me that they
were not going to do anything for Terry Lowery, and they kept
their word.

I am a licensed clinical social worker, and have been a
social worker for more than 45 years and I cannot begin to
count the number of times that I have tried to get legal help for
my former clients, only to find out that they did not qualify for
legal aid or the federally funded, Legal Services. Some people
criticize the poor for staying poor, but there are many reasons
that people are in poverty. I grew up poor, but since I lived in
a depressed area, almost everyone was poor, so I never thought
of myself as being very impoverished. There are as many
reasons for people being poor, as there are for reasons why
people are rich. Some people who are born into poverty stay
poor because of defective parenting, and addictions. Others
remain poor due to lack of education, or lack of motivation
due to false self messages passed onto them by others, which
the individual chooses to believe about themselves. There are
large numbers of poor people who are sick, and many of them
are that way because they grew up poor, and did not get the
medical attention that they needed, especially the preventative
type. One of my former jobs as a social worker was in a medical
clinic for the poor in upstate New York. There I saw, first
hand, the large number of people who were poor because of
medical problems.

Many of my former clients had need of legal help, and
most of them had to depend on public defenders to present
their cases to the courts. They could not choose which public

defender they wanted. An attorney was assigned to them. Sometimes they would get a good lawyer who would fight for them, and other times their assigned lawyer would do as little as possible, and seemingly fight against them.

Terry was fortunate to get a good state appointed public defender when he went to get a Post Conviction Relief, as it was called, who succeeded in getting him off of Death Row. However, after he was off of Death Row, over the course of many years, I hired two different law firms. The first group of lawyers promised a lot of things, but just took our money, and then said there was nothing they could do. The second one did essentially the same thing.

I hired the second lawyer when DNA first came out, and was found to positively trace crimes back to the perpetrators. He seemed like a nice guy, and I thought he was a good lawyer until he went to present Terry's case to the judge. He promised us that he would get DNA testing done for Terry, and he assured us that Terry could be exonerated. Then when it came time to go to court that lawyer petitioned the judge to exhume the body of the victim, and that was where Terry's case ended. That action irritated the judge in Fort Wayne, and all future chances for release were thwarted. Later on that lawyer fled the country and went to live in Australia, leaving many cases unresolved. Also, he took money from people who had paid him without him providing services for them.

It is no secret that corruption is spurred on by those who peddle back room and under the table bribes in our criminal justice system. When I worked for the Welfare Department at the county courthouse I witnessed how lawyers and county officials operated. Lawyers would argue vehemently against other lawyers, and then go out to lunch or have cocktails with each other afterwards. It is like a sporting game to them in which two teams fight each other on the football field, and then go up and shake hands afterwards.

Former governor George Ryan of the state of Illinois helped renew the national debate about capital punishment in the year 2000. According to Wikipedia he said, "We have now freed more people than we have put to death under our system." "There is a flaw in the system, without question, and it needs to be studied."

> "On January 11, 2003, just two days before leaving office, Ryan commuted (to life terms) the sentences of everyone on or waiting to be sent to Death Row—a total of 167 convicts due to his belief that the death penalty could not be administered fairly."

After leaving office Ryan became an inmate himself when he was charged and convicted of scandals which involved some of his former employees and friends. According to Wikipedia:

> "Ryan's political career was marred by a scandal called, 'Operation Safe Road', which involved the illegal sale of government licenses, contracts and leases by state employees during his prior service as Secretary of State. In the wake of numerous convictions of his former aides, he chose not to run for reelection in 2002. Seventy-nine former state officials, lobbyists, and others were charged in the investigation, and at least 76 were convicted."

> "The corruption scandal leading to Ryan's downfall began more than a decade earlier

during a federal investigation into a deadly crash in Wisconsin. Six children from the Willis family of Chicago, Illinois, were killed, their parents, Rev. Duane and Janet Willis were severely burned. The investigation revealed a scheme inside of Ryan's Secretary of State's office in which unqualified truck drivers obtained licenses through bribes."

"The former governor was released from federal prison last July 3, 2013 after serving five years for corruption in a case spurred by the 1994 highway crash that killed six children of Scott and Janet Willis. The tragedy dominated Ryan's trial as the truck driver who caused the accident had received a license through a bribe from a staffer in Ryan's office when he was Secretary of State"

I guess the story about Judge Ryan goes to show several points that this writer is trying to make. A once honorable judge saw injustices in the court system being done, and tried to correct them, while at the same time, he was either not aware of what his employees were doing, or knew it, allowed it, and contributed to it. The other possibility is that he was framed by disgruntled colleagues. There is always another side to a story. Far be it for me to judge a judge.

There is an agency that was founded in 1992 by lawyers, Barry Scheck and Peter Neufeld at the Cardozo School of law that has freed 362 people to date who were convicted of crimes they did not commit. The average prison time spent for those who have been exonerated was 14 years. Most of them were freed because of DNA testing. The name of that agency is the Innocence Project.

Here is some information gleaned from their website:

> "As the pace of DNA exonerations has grown across the country in recent year, wrongful convictions have revealed disturbing fissures and trends in our criminal justice system. Together these cases show us how the criminal justice system is broken—and how urgently it needs to be fixed."

> "We should learn from the system failures. In each case where DNA has proven innocence beyond doubt, an overlapping array of contributing factors has emerged from mistakes, to misconduct, to factors of race and class."

The Innocence Project goes on to list the common causes of errors that they have found present in the cases that have gotten overturned and/or exonerated. These are some of them:

- Eyewitness Misidentification
- False Confessions or Admissions
- Government Misconduct
- Unvalidated or Improper Forensic Science
- Informants
- Inadequate Defense

In Terry's case all of the above errors were present, and all of them, plus a biased press, contributed to his conviction. The only other person at the murder scene was the boy whose girlfriend was the victim, and who was the only one with a motive. Terry had no relationship with the young girl. Terry was forced to confess by police torture. He had always been victimized since he was 2 years old, so it was easy for the police to brain wash him into a confession because he was used to being accused of things he did not do, and forced to do things that he did not want to do. Also, the public was wanting someone to get punished, and the police were under pressure to catch someone and make an example out of them to improve their image. I believe that this is a very important factor. Police are under a lot of pressure from the public, the media, and their superiors to solve crimes, and get convictions, one way or the other.

It was common knowledge at that period of time in Indiana that Fort Wayne was a dangerous city to even visit, let alone live in. Several friends have told me that when they were teenagers and young adults they were advised to stay away from Fort Wayne because of the high crime rate, and unsolved crimes there.

At the time of the investigation the police never tested the substance on Terry's clothes, or they would have found that it was Rustolium, (a substance that was used as a paint primer for cars). The only informant was the other defendant who got to the police before Terry did, and his family was able to afford a private lawyer. Terry had a public defender who was hired by the court who wanted to convict him to show the public they could catch criminals and solve crimes. Public defenders were not paid very much back in those days either, so they had little incentive to spend much time working on those type of cases.

I had first met Terry in the spring of 1986. After our first face to face visit I continued to write him, visit him, send him scriptures, and other information which I thought would boost his spirits. I also talked about him to my friends and found other people in the community who were interested in prisoners, and took them with me to visit Terry. Over the next

7 years Terry and I got to be very good friends. He encouraged me as much as I encouraged him. He convinced me that I had what it took to go back to school and get my master's degree in social work, which is what I did.

When I told my then husband that I had applied to graduate school, and was accepted at Indiana University/ Purdue University in Indianapolis, the first words out of his mouth were, "Let's get a divorce". The next day he came home from work and told me that he knew of a way we could fund my graduate school. While I was very grateful that he was then willing to help me go back to school, there was this thought in the back of my mind that he really didn't want me to further my education for some reason or another. So, when I went to graduate school I rented an apartment in Indianapolis, where I stayed during the week and came home on the weekends. That way I had easy access to campus, and was able to study without interruptions. I found that I enjoyed living by myself and making my own decisions, even if it was only part-time. When I graduated and it was time to give up my apartment, I was sad to do so because it meant going back and living with my alcoholic husband, who could say some pretty damaging things, mostly about my intellect, and my faith. He had known me since high school when I was known for saying the wrong things at the right time to get laughs from my peers. Therefore, he would make jokes about me, which I thought were no longer funny, as I had long since grown up, and viewed his sarcastic jokes as insults into the very core of my being.

Due to the fact that my marriage was going sour, and I was unhappy and tired of being emotionally abused by my husband, I was very vulnerable to the kindness and appreciation shown to me by Terry. He would tell me that my husband did not know what he had, and he would tell me that I was intelligent, beautiful, and much more capable than I ever thought I was.

Also, he told me that he loved me. I threatened to stop seeing him if he didn't stop saying those things, but then I relented, and told myself that I could handle a crush, and not let it affect me. That is why when during one of our visits I was surprised, and shocked when this overwhelming revelation came to me that I was in love with this man. I tried to deny it, repress it, forget about it, but it was like I was hit with a lightning bolt. I did not plan it or want it to happen, and I never believed other people in the past who said that they "fell in love" with someone instantly like that before. But, that is what happened to me. I felt I had to tell someone. I had no one I could tell to get some counseling from. Since I was in graduate school at that time, I was afraid that if I sought counseling they would kick me out of graduate school. Since there was no one I could talk to about the matter, I told Terry. From that point on it was a love I could not deny. I knew it wasn't right to be in love with someone I was not married to, but I knew my marriage had been going downhill for a long time, and I had been trying to hold it together while the kids were growing up because I did not want my kids being raised by someone else, or have them go through the trauma that I had seen my sister's children, and many others go through. At that point in my life my children were adults, and I did not think a divorce or separation would affect them that much. They knew what I had been through, and had put up with from their father, and I thought they would understand. They didn't.

My husband had also found someone else, and I came home one day and found a woman sitting on his lap in my living room. Both of them were asleep. That seemed to settle it. When I moved out, and got an apartment in Kokomo, she stayed. We got a divorce the following year, and I married Terry while he was still on Death Row.

CHAPTER 4

Our wedding was not like normal weddings. I was allowed to wear a nice dress. It was just a white lacy dress that was of average street length, not a traditional wedding dress. They brought Terry in with an orange jumpsuit on, and both his hands and feet were shackled. Also, they had a chain around his waist that was shackled to the shackle on his ankles. (I don't know where they thought he was going to go with guards all around, and behind locked doors.) Nevertheless, Terry was grinning from ear to ear, and so was I. Terry had arranged for us to use a room outside of the Death Row area that was usually used for parole hearings. Terry and I had a mutual friend who stood up for him as his best person, (She was female), and I had a good friend of mine as my matron of honor by the name of Debbie. His appeal lawyer's husband was the minister who presided over our wedding. We had written our own vows, and the pastor added his words to the ceremony. The thing I cherished the most about our wedding was the fact that my new husband cried at our wedding. Despite the happiness of that day, getting married on Death Row does not foretell a happy future. After the wedding I provided a luncheon at a nearby restaurant for my friends, but, of course, Terry was not there. That was in March of 1993.

In 1994, Terry's case went back to court for what was called a post-conviction release. What happened that day in court was very interesting. Terry was taken to the Fort Wayne County Jail from the prison, and then was placed in a holding cell in the basement of the county courthouse on the day of the hearing. I was sitting in the reception area of the prosecutor's office while Terry's state appointed lawyer, the prosecutor, and two other lawyers went into an inner office, and worked out a proposal that Terry was later advised to sign. We must have waited a couple of hours for the proposal to be typed up before Terry was brought up from the basement, and we all went into another conference room where the lawyers, the prosecutor, Terry, myself, and a couple of police officers were seated. The lawyers presented us with the document, they had composed and said that it was the best deal we could get, and if we did not sign it, and opted for a second jury trial, it might cost us at least, $50,000.00, and if he lost it the second time, he would never get out. (Later, I thought that a person cannot be charged twice for the same crime, but at the time, that question never crossed my mind.) Also, if he accepted the proposal, the death sentence would be overturned and he would be given 60 years in prison instead, with time off for good behavior.

There was nothing in that form in which he had to admit guilt. Not wanting to gamble with Terry's life, we accepted the proposal, and his death sentence was vacated. We were not given any private time to look over the form, and we felt pressured to sign it there and then with all of those people looking on.

Unnoticed to us at the time, and not mentioned to us by any of the lawyers was a few words that sealed his fate for a long time, and kept him from being able to effectively fight for and/or obtain an earlier release was this *sneaky statement:*

> "THE PETITIONER IS FOREVER BARRED BY HIS EXPRESS WAIVER FROM ASSERTING ANY CLAIM FOR RELIEF FROM THIS PROSECUTION AND CONVICTION."

Of course the above statement, and especially the words, *"Forever Barred"* were not in large print on the paper he signed. Also, at the time we were both under a lot of duress with having to make a life changing decision quickly, without having adequate time to look over the document, and having lawyers, and police officers pressuring us to make a decision. We were led to believe that if new evidence was found, it was possible that we could still lose the case, and there would never be a chance for him to get out. It seemed that all the cards were stacked against us, and we never saw, and none of our lawyers pointed out the, "Forever Barred" statement. The little hope that we were given proved to be false hope because a judge or a court can interpret the law any way that they choose whether one agrees with it or not.

After making that agonizing decision another very interesting thing happened. The court was assembled, complete with lawyers for the defense, the family of the victim, and the judge. There were even uninvolved onlookers in the gallery. All of this occurred within an hour or two after Terry signed the papers. People who are more familiar with court proceedings than I am said that it is very unusual for court hearing to take place that quickly, on the same day that a court document is composed and signed. Most of the court hearings that I have been involved with, in my work, are scheduled weeks in advance, and if postponed can be scheduled months away. My perception of why they hurried up the court hearing the way they did was that so we would not have time to change our minds, and the public would not be notified of what was happening in court that day. Terry's case was heavily publicized at the time of his trial and conviction.

Being married to a man in prison is not the best kind of life, but we survived it by looking forward to the day when he would get out, and the next time he could phone or we would see each other. Of course, he had to call collect, and those calls were very expensive. Depending on the facility that he was in we could talk from about 15 to 30 minutes at a time, and each call was subject to monitoring, and we were rudely cut off when the time was up. If we were lucky he could call back, and I would get charged for another call. The prisons profit from each of those calls, and families of prisoners who are already financially strained get punished if they want to hear from their loved ones.

During the time that Terry was in prison I continued to work as an outpatient psychotherapist, and met with many people who had similar experiences with the justice system that Terry and I were having.

CHAPTER 5

John's Story

One such person was a middle aged man, who I will call, John. (His name has been changed for confidentiality) John was a divorced man who had a daughter with his ex-wife. After his divorce from his wife she accused him of molesting their daughter when he had a parental visit. Since the girl was only 5 at the time, the ex-wife coerced her daughter to say that her daddy had molested her. Consequently, John got convicted of child molestation, and sent to prison for about 7 years. In the past when a child said they had been molested, the court believed them, under the belief that a child would not lie about such a thing. When the daughter grew up she admitted that she had been coerced to say that her dad had molested her, admitted that he had not done so, and she became very close to him as an adult. However, the damage had already been done, and his life was ruined.

John is not alone. There are many men who have been falsely accused of child molestation by angry women, who try to get revenge for one reason or another. Those men can have their lives destroyed for no reason other than choosing the wrong woman to have children with.

If a person is a convicted child molester it is believed that they will never be able to heal from that problem, and they have to register with the sheriff's department every year, and they cannot live near a school or a playground. Also, in our county there is a weekly newspaper that prints the pictures of everyone who gets arrested, and what they are arrested for. For child molesters, they post their pictures in a special issue, at certain times of the year. Please don't think I am defending real child molesters. I believe child molesting or any kind of mistreatment of children is despicable. I am talking about those who have been wrongly accused that should always be taken into consideration. Also, it is very hard to have real evidence after the incident or incidents have happened. Investigators have to rely on circumstantial evidence, as well as what the child says, and how the child has been acting. How many of us know that children can sometimes lie?

CHAPTER 6

Adam's Story

Once again the name has been changed to protect the person being spoken about, but it is a true story. Adam grew up in a one parent family in the bad part of a big city. When he became a teenager, the school he was in had a lot of gangs, so he decided to protect himself by taking a knife to school. The school found the knife, and sent him to a juvenile work camp where he got in with more boys who were in gangs, and when he came out of the work camp he was worse off than he was before going there. He got in trouble again, and was sent off to a correctional facility for boys for a couple of years. Meanwhile, his mother decided that it would be better to move to a different state, thinking that maybe her son would have a better chance if he got away from his gang members. When Adam got out of Boy's School, and joined his mother in another state he got in trouble again at the new location, and was sent to prison this time, since he was now an adult. Adam's family were all strong Christians, so he knew right from wrong, but at that time in his life he had not learned how to do the right things. His father was a part time father who had a affinity for guns, and liked to drink so his mother would not marry him.

After a couple of short prison terms Adam was released and determined to do the right thing, so he married a woman who had a troubled background like his, thinking that they had a lot in common, and they both started going to church. He had two children by that woman, and things went well for a year or two. Then he discovered that his wife was cheating on him, and was also selling her body, and was working as an exotic dancer when he was at work. When Adam decided he could not tolerate her antics any more he filed for divorce. It was then that he had more problems than he had ever had in his life because now he had two lovely children to think about. He loved his two little children, but found that when they were with their mother they were not being properly taken care of. In fact, they were being neglected, and he had reports from relatives that they had found the children locked inside a room for several hours at a time to fend for themselves without supervision, when they were only 2 and 3 years of age. Because of Adam's history, his ex-wife was able to convince Child Protection that she was the better parent, and he was the one who was not capable of taking care of the children. The courts and the child protection services in that community were determined to give that mother, who had had 4 other children taken away from her in the past for neglect, chance after chance despite evidence to the contrary that she had been using drugs, prostituting, putting lewd pictures of herself on Face Book, and neglecting the children when she had them. When Adam would go to pick up the children they would be dirty, and would be wearing diapers that had not been changed in a long time. His ex-wife was even seen driving away in a car whose occupant shot a gun through his girlfriend's window, almost hitting her child.

It took two years of multiple court battles for Adam to get permanent custody of his children. Even after he had custody, he had to take his ex-wife back to court twice because she kept violating every court order there was when she had visitations with them. She was so good at manipulating people that even her own mother did not trust her.

After several years in which Adam had to pay lawyers, and court costs, as well as pay child support, he was able to convince the court that he was a good father, and should have primary custody of his children. Even then he was not able to limit visitations with the mother because the caseworkers in that county keep trying to give that wayward woman chance after chance to change her ways.

Are there different rules for fathers than for mothers in the Justice System? In Adam's case it surely appears that there was. Was he being judged because he had a prison record, even after he had proven himself to be law abiding? Of course he was. Why wasn't his ex-wife judged for her criminal behavior for so long of a time? My guess is that she might have had some kind of a connection someone in authority there, as I have seen happen in other situations.

CHAPTER 7

Rachel's Story

Another client, who I will call Rachel, told me about a situation in which she had been injured in a car accident, and the doctor had given her some strong pain medicine to alleviate the pain. Knowing that she had some strong medicine, a person, who she thought was a friend, gave her a sob story about her boyfriend who did not have a doctor to prescribe medicine for him, and wanted to buy some of her pain medicine. Rachel was a law abiding person, and one who was sympathetic to the pain of other people, and she told the woman she would just give her some of the pills for her friend because she wasn't interested in selling them to her. The other party asked her if she was aware that she could get money for those pills, and my client again said that she was not interested in making money off of her medicine. When the woman said her boyfriend was willing to pay her $50.00 for 5 pills. Finally, my client agreed to do it, not thinking that she was doing anything wrong.

My client then found out too late that the Woman who talked her into accepting money for the pain pills was told by the police that if she could tape record someone accepting money for pain pills her boyfriend would be released from jail. The former friend of my client, ie informant, was wearing a wire when she talked my client into selling her the pills, which were probably some kind of Opiates, and the informant recorded the transaction so that she could free her boyfriend, while betraying her friend.

My client was stunned when the police arrested her and she had to serve 18 months of home detention for trying to help out a friend. One would think that the court could see, by the recording, that she thought that she was helping her friend out, and was talked into something she did not really want to do.

My question here is, why was a police officer so desperate to convict someone that he had to bribe someone to trick another person into, unknowingly, commit a crime? Are police officers pressured to bring in suspects?

CHAPTER 8

Jay's Story

Another former client, who I will call, Jay, tape recorded a sad story which forever changed his life. It brought tears to his eyes even years later as he told about mistakes he had made by marrying the wrong woman. Here is his story.

"In 1984 I met a girl named, Kathy, and a couple of weeks later we ended up in bed. That was on Halloween, and about six weeks later she told me she was pregnant with my child. In December I married her, wanting to do the right thing, and marry her. After about 8 months she confessed that the baby was not my child, and the real father was on drugs, and there was a possibility that the baby was going to be deformed. So, being the person that I was, young and stupid, I freaked out because I didn't know how I was going to take care of a deformed child, or how I would have the money, the resources, and etc. My wife wanted to give the child up for adoption, but when I saw my daughter after she was born, I just couldn't do it. She came out perfectly healthy. Next thing I knew we were having marital problems, and she came to me and told me she was in an occult.

Different things were not adding up, and I knew I had to get away from this woman because of everything that was going on. She was then pregnant with my son, Brian, and he was born in September of 1985. She told me that if I ever divorced her that I would have to play hell in seeing these kids. At the time I didn't know what she meant by that, and when I finally found out what she meant by that, it was too late.

I moved away to Orlando because my job laid me off. I was in Orlando for nine months working, and did not see my kids. I met another young woman named, Paula, married her, and she helped me take care of the kids, once I moved back to my home town, and got my former job back. At that time I was getting visitations with my kids, but then all of a sudden the visitations would come and go. She would make excuses saying that they were sick, or something was up, or stuff like that. So I had to start taking her to court.

After I would take the children back home I started getting calls from the Welfare Dept. asking me if I had molested my children in anyway shape or form. I just laughed at them and told them they were nuts, and hung up. Little did I realize that Kathy was taking my daughter, Michelle, to the hospital after each time they visited me, and having a rape test done on her. I also learned that Kathy was stripping down my daughter in front of two other adults, spreading her vagina, and showing them that she still had her hymen. To this day, my daughter still believes I had done something to her because her mother convinced her I did.

We went to court when my daughter was 4 and my son was 3, and the children testified that I held a knife to them, and if I didn't get my way, I would cut them, which, NO. I never did that.(My client said that he was not allowed in the Court room during that trial, and was told that if he was in the court room it would intimidate the children, he could not refute the charges). As soon as I gave up my rights as a father, all the charges were dropped, and nothing more was ever said or done."

"My son is now 30, and I just started seeing him, after 25 years. My daughter, I saw at my youngest daughter's wedding this past week. The only other time I had seen her was when my younger daughter graduated six years ago."

"At one time when I was going through my divorce with Kathy, and we went before a judge in a town in Indiana. That judge threatened Kathy that he would give me full custody if I did not get visitation rights. That judge was able to get Kathy to confess that it was her, and not me who had been molesting the children. The judge wanted to go to Madison County and testify that in the Madison County Court, but Madison County would not let him, saying that, "This is not your jurisdiction, stay out of it. We need to prosecute this guy, and we will."

"While I was going through those custody proceedings I would get a call every day from the Madison County Welfare Dept. saying that they had proof, and that they were going to put me away in prison, and for me to give up my father's rights. These were daily phone calls, either at my job, or at my residence. I told them to bring it on, and if they could show me proof that I had done such a thing, they wouldn't have to send me to jail, I would go myself because I know that is wrong, and I know right from wrong. Their harassment wore on me so bad that at one point they had me convinced that I had done it. When I went to complain to the Welfare, my complaint fell on deaf ears. They did nothing about it, except to increase the phone calls, and increase the intensity of the interrogation. After I got my attorney the calls stopped. In fact, I was told that one of the Welfare caseworkers got fired for the harassment. Then the prosecutor from Madison County told my attorney, "We know he is innocent, but we still have to prosecute because the state wants us to do that".

"At one point I had to check into a mental hospital because I knew that I did not molest my daughter, but with all the harassment and mental abuse they halfway convinced me that I did what I didn't do. I had to sort out my thoughts in a safe place so that I could think clearly, and realistically." (That was when he sought counseling, and when I first got to be acquainted with him.)

"When the Welfare Department fired the lady who had been doing the harassing phone calls, I got another caseworker who listened to me. I kept telling her, 'Please check the medical records. Go to the hospital, and look at the records to see if they found that anything had been done when they did all of those rape kits. Go to the doctor. She was not being molested, and th e caseworker did as I asked her to do'. Then that caseworker took the information she had found to the prosecuting attorney.

Then the prosecuting attorney again told my attorney that they knew I was innocent, but the state wants us to prosecute this guy anyway. He said that he was very sorry, but they had no choice, but if he would give up his rights as a father, then we could make this all go away. Since I was not in the courtroom that day, when my attorney came out he said that I had a 50/50 gamble here, and asked me, 'What do you want to do'? I asked him what he meant by that, and he said that if you go through with this, you might end up in prison, but if you give up your rights as a father, the prosecutor will make it all go away."

"So, as hard as it was for me, I gave up my rights as a father, and I have regretted it ever since. I wish I would have worked a little bit harder, and maybe I would have had a better relationship with my kids today. At that time when the attorney presented the options to me, I had to give him a decision right then, that day. I didn't have time to think about it. I had to have an answer right then. It was not a 24 hour decision. He had to have the answer right then, so I signed over my rights as a father. To this day, I have had background checks, and nothing has ever shown up on my records that I am a child molester, or anything about what the Welfare Dept. did to me back in those days".

In all of the cases mentioned above grave injustices were done to common people who were not knowledgeable about the justice system, and the people who held powerful positions until they had to learn the hard way, by trial and error. Our laws started with the Ten Commandments, and then our government set up a legal standard, based on the Ten Commandments, which our forefathers developed into the United States Constitution, and the Bill of Rights. I uphold the laws of this country, and am a very patriotic citizen. However, the interpretation, and implementation of our laws have been very badly skewed because people, in places of authority, have been able to do whatever they can get away with because the process of challenging injustices for many of us is not available, not affordable, or made clear to the general public.

I believe the statutes are not clear to the general public in much the same way that many of us have to get some kind of experts to complete our income tax forms. The laws are written in what I call, Legalese, so that only lawyers can understand them. I guess that every profession has its' own jargon. Doctors and nurses have terms that most of us cannot even read, let alone pronounce or spell. Psychologists and social worker have some professional jargon too. However, when it pertains to legal matters, ones freedom can be taken away, sometimes without the person knowing what they did wrong.

My objective in pointing out injustices in the justice system is not to promote anarchy or say that the people who commit crimes should not be punished. I believe that a civilized society has to have high standards to solve and punish real criminals who are guilty of the crimes they are accused of. What I am saying is that everyone, regardless of income, knowledge, social status, or influence should be given equal opportunities to be defended for what they are accused of. As it is now our legal system is prone to biases. Biases by victims, biases by the policing authorities, and biases by the prosecutors, lawyers, judges, and, yes, by public welfare agencies. I have witnessed a lot of damage that has been done by public welfare agencies, by seemingly, well meaning people. There should never be a time when "The state, or the prosecutor, or the public says they are guilty, so we have to prosecute them". Each person should be given the right to be judged by solid evidence, not hearsay, opinion, or whether or not they look guilty from their past history.

CHAPTER 9

Our Lives while Terry was in Prison

The prison system moved Terry around from one prison to another several times. In his 26 years in prison he was moved 5 times. Each prison in the same state had a different set of rules. The last prison he was in was only 15 miles from home. That one was called, Miami Correctional. While he was there he was able to enroll in college courses because Grace College, and Ball State University set up a program with the prison in which they would send professors from their colleges to instruct those who were willing, able, and eligible to be educated at a college level. Through that program Terry was able to get a Bachelor's degree in Business, with a minor in Biblical studies. Later on, at that same facility, he got into a program called, The Plus Program. That program was put on by local volunteers from different churches that would go to the prison, and help the inmates learn how to adjust to the free world, once they were released from prison.

One of the volunteers was a man by the name of Lonnie Henderson. Lon became a friend of the inmates. When he would go into the group at the prison the men would line up to get a hug from Lon. He was well loved by everyone, and made a huge difference in the lives of the men there. Lon took a special interest in Terry, and when Terry got out of prison he hired him to help with different projects around his house. We became friends with both Lon and his wife Janet, who are wonderful people. Lon taught Terry a lot about carpentry, as well as how to be patient. He also taught him and the other inmates about the Christian faith by both words and the way he lived.

After serving 26 years in prison for a crime that he did not commit, Terry was finally released on March 12th, 2011. He worked his way out of prison and rehabilitated himself by working every job he could get, taking advantage of every program he could learn from that had a time cut connected to it, and by staying out of trouble. Terry tried to do the right things, did a lot of praying, stayed away from the trouble makers, and never joined a gang. He had no respect for gang members.

During the time that Terry was in prison I often felt like I was in prison too. To cope with my lonesome life, I wrapped myself up in my work, went to church, had a small circle of friends, and wrote to Terry, and visited him every two weeks. One of the ways I found to fight off loneliness was to share my home with other single women who needed a temporary home. A couple of the women stayed with me a year or two, and it was nice to have their companionship. The last woman who stayed with me, convinced me to never to open up my home to a boarder again. She did not have a job, but she had a rich mother. Every day she would go shopping, and she started filling up the house with items that I did not have room for. One night she hung up on a phone call from my husband, which nearly broke us up. Then, on another occasion she told my husband that if we ever broke up, he could come and live with her. That was the final straw, and I helped to find her a house to buy, and gave her my old car to get her to move out. I have never heard from her again.

One really good thing happened while Terry was located in a prison called, Wabash Valley, which is located in southwestern Indiana. One winter night when I was walking out of the prison, there was another lady who was leaving at the same time. We struck up a conversation while we were walking to our cars, and decided to meet at a restaurant that was located not far from the prison. We seemed to become friends immediately, and learned that we lived in the same part of the state, so we decided to share rides to and from the prison, since she was visiting her boyfriend there also. Her name is Debi, and she and I are still friends to this day.

There were many times when Terry was in prison that he would tell me about problems which he could not fix on his own, so I would run interference for him by calling the Dept. of Correction, or the prison officials to try to get his problem resolved. Many times he would ask me to help other inmates whose relatives were not able to see them, or their families had not contacted them. I would call them, and sometimes I even took their family members up to the prison with me, and, of course took them home afterwards. Sometimes there would be health issues, and sanitation issues inside the prison, and I would call the health department and report the problems to them. A lot of times Terry would not get his medicine when he should have, and I had to call the prison and complain. Terry has tachycardia, and he cannot go without his medicine, but many times the prison would let him get down to 0 pills before they would renew his meds, and by that time he would be hurting and anxious.

One time I went to visit him, and he was really sick. He had been trying to get someone to let him see a nurse for a couple of days, but they kept ignoring him. I called one of the guards over to our table while we were sitting in the visiting room, and told him the problem, and said, 'Look at him, he has a fever, and has been sick for several days now, and has not gotten to see a doctor or nurse'. Because I demanded that something be done, the guard took him to the infirmary right then. Otherwise, who knows how long it would have been before he got medical attention. Many inmates have no one on the outside who will advocate for them. Many families of inmates are afraid of complaining to the guards or anyone.

Every time he was eligible Terry would apply for clemency, and each time we would go in front of the Parole or Clemency Board,(which are the same as they have the same people on both), I would prepare a lengthy presentation stating all the reasons why Terry deserved to be released. One year, 2007, he did not get to file for clemency because the clemency papers, which had been filled out in plenty of time, got lost within the prison system. In 2008 the same thing happened, and I tried to find out what happened to them and no explanations were ever given as to why those petitions just dissolved into thin air. The Department of Correction and the entire justice system polices itself, and to my knowledge, there is no "neutral agency" that oversees what they, the courts, the states, and all the way up to the supreme court does, unless it is bad enough to be picked up by The FBI, or a Senate Sub-committee. One could say that the public oversees local, state, and federal agencies, but the public is not aware of what goes on in many agencies unless someone openly complains.

In 1996 Terry got an anonymous letter from someone who said that they had been at a party where the co-defendant in his court case was, and whose girlfriend was the victim in the crime Terry was serving time for. The anonymous letter was an admission of committing the crime.

The anonymous letter was of no help at all. All the officials and lawyers we showed it to said that Terry could have written it himself, or had someone else write it for him. They never tried to check out the handwriting or the paper it was written on because they already had a conviction, and did not care if they had the right man or not.

Before Terry got into a bona fide College when he was at Miami Correctional, he tried to get an education through some correspondence schools. He did get a certified GED through International Correspondence School, but when he first tried to get a college degree by correspondence he found a correspondence school which seemed legitimate, but turned out not to be. That school promised to use life time experience as a substitute for some classes, and they scammed $3000. from us. One of his class assignments was to summarize a couple books of the Bible. Terry decided that he would summarize the entire Bible, which he did. After he finished doing that one of my friends and I typed it up, and when it was finished we sent it in. When we didn't hear anything back from the school, I checked up on it, and found that they were found to be fraudulent, so we lost our money, and all the time and effort that we all had put into the project.

As mentioned before, after my first divorce and marriage to Terry I bought half of a duplex in town, had a few friends, lost a few friends, focused on my work, wrote to Terry, and looked forward to his calls and our next visit. We usually got our pictures taken when we had a visit, and having those to look at was a great help. Terry would draw pictures, and got very good at doing oil paintings, and pastels which I was able to bring home, and have framed. At some prisons I was able to send him some art supplies, and at others that was not allowed. Since Terry is a very good musician I also bought him a complete drum set, guitars, amplifiers, and etc. Terry helped pay for the drum set, but he did not make much money in prison.

Most people don't know it, but there are private industries in prisons which take advantage of the cheap labor that the inmates can provide. Terry worked for several of them, and learned how to make mattresses, and garments for the prisoners. He liked to stay busy, and still does. The inmates wages often depend on what level the prisoner is at any given time. If they are in a lower level they make only about .50 or.70 cents an hour. As they move up they can make minimum wage, which to them is good pay.

We did everything we could to hasten his release, and prepare him for life outside in society. I took friends I knew up to meet him. I found people who were interested in prison ministry, and took some of them to meet him. I wanted to familiarize him with the good people since all he had known was the other kind.

I took a couple of pastors up to meet him, and one or two of them went to see them on their own at least once. One couple from a church I was going to became really close friends with both of us. Martin even attended a couple of the Clemency hearings and gave a positive testimony on Terry's behalf. One of the pastors did that also. Martin and Jan were very supportive to both of us, and helped out whenever they could.

When Terry was released my pastor at the time, Pastor Tim Brown, and his wife Dawn were at our house to welcome him. I had to work that day, and could not be home. They took a video of that day's events. It was like Christmas for Terry because he had a 14 piece drum set 2 guitars, an amplifier, new clothes, and everything he needed to start a new life in the free world. Most inmates are lucky to have a place to live when they get out.

CHAPTER 10

Terry's Prison Traumas

While he was in prison Terry did not tell me too much of the gory details of some of the things that he experienced, and witnessed while he was incarcerated. Perhaps he was afraid that it would sicken me, or maybe he just wanted to forget it. Whatever the reason, the following is his verbatim account of some of the things he witnessed, in his own words.

> "There were so many things that happened in there, things that one can only remotely imagine. In prison a person sees a lot of different things. I guess it has affected me in a lot of different ways, and a lot of things that I seen kind of haunt me some. In 26 years in prison I saw people cut, stabbed, burned, and guards abusing people. At one time they even killed

somebody in there. I remember walking past someone's cell and seeing them dead with a needle stuck in their arm, or them hanging in their cell. I remember one time I got up early one morning for breakfast, and they opened the bar, (that locked all the doors), and there was this guy in a wheelchair outside of my cell who just slumped over on the floor. The guards talked it over, called the nurse, and she didn't bring anything with her, no stethoscope, no oxygen, and they had to keep running back and forth to get things. The thing is, he was already dead because I have seen it before. No matter how or when a person dies, according to the D.O.C., 'They died on the way to the hospital'. I remember one morning at Michigan City Prison when I used to work in the tag shop, (licensplates). You got all kinds of different people that work in there, like drug dealers, murderers, rapists, child molesters, snitches. On the range, (levels of cell blocks), was this guy who was always telling on people for stuff, and even the guards didn't like him because he was always telling on people. One morning someone brought in a 5 gallon bucket of what we called white gas. It was a thinner that we used in the print shop to make the license plates. Then one guy walked past his cell and threw it in on him. We could hear the guy cussing, and everything. Then a guy came behind the first guy with a book of matches. He lit them, and threw that in on him. We could hear this *whoosh* sound, people screaming, and the smell of fire. Some people were saying, 'kill the fucking snitch'. Others were saying, 'Let the mother fucker die'. We could hear that guy in the cell screaming like you couldn't even imagine, and the smell of burning flesh is something you don't ever forget. The whole cell house was full of smoke. All the guards came in. The riot squad and everybody was locked in their rooms, and stuff. They tried to open the cell the guy was in, but they couldn't because the bars were too hot. When they did bring him down on a gurney, they didn't even cover him up. I guess they wanted everybody else to see it. When you see it all, you can't even imagine."

"I remember another time when I was in C Cell House in Michigan City. A couple of guys got into it over something. Out here there are things that we think don't even matter. But in there even a cigarette is a big deal. They got into it for some reason, and one guy pulled out a shank, (a homemade weapon), and put it into the other guy's gut, and split him open from one side to the other. His whole insides fell out on the floor. There was blood everywhere, and his intestines were lying on the floor. The nurses and doctors tried to put his insides back in him by tying him up with a sheet. They backed the ambulance up to the prison, which was something they never do, and like everyone else, 'He died on the way to the hospital'.

Then there was the time on Death Row when this guy named Mark, was supposed to prove himself to somebody, and he had a toothbrush with a razor blade melted onto it. He went a after this guy, and started slicing him. He sliced his head, his face, his arm. Man, he just cut him to pieces. We came to find out that the guy was rapping on his case. Some of the things I seen in there."

"One morning I had problems with this one guy. They were wanting to start their own little gang on Death Row. I have never been one to join a gang. One guy came in my cell with some scalding hot water, and threw it on me because I would not join their little club."

(Terry got 3rd degree burns from that incident, and had to be treated by the medical staff by having them peel off the top layers of skin to let the skin underneath heal. He was also put in segregation after that to keep him safe from the people who did the scalding, while he healed. Terry told me at the time that he got off one good punch at the guy who scalded him, as the skin was falling off of his arm. Due to the fact that Terry fought back, he got a disciplinary charge filed against him, which said nothing about the fact that he fought back in self-defense.

"My chest was just a mess, and as they walked me over to Medical, the skin was falling off of my chest. It was really cold out, but with the heat of that burn, the cold air felt good. There were days of going through being debrided. That was something else."

"There was another time when this little old guy went over to Medical because he was having a hard time breathing. His name was Angel. He was a little old Mexican guy who probably didn't weigh more than a 100 lbs. The guards over there grabbed hold of him, out of the sight of the cameras, and we found out that they ended up suffocating him to death. They transferred the guards out for awhile until they got the heat off of them. One guard was not even a sergeant when he left, but he came back to the prison as a sergeant. Nothing ever happened to them. Whenever there were any incidents involving the guards at the prison, they would always get together, and get their stories straight so they were never to blame. It was always the inmates fault. The guards themselves were no different than we were."

"The guards would bring in weed. Some of the female guards would sell themselves for money. The guards would bring in drugs, cell phones, and whatever else. I admit I had a lady guard bring me in tobacco, and she was dealing with a lot of different people, so she kept books to keep herself straight. One time someone dropped a note on her because they didn't get whatever it was that they wanted fast enough. The guards were waiting for her up front when she came in. They patted her down, and found tobacco, lighters, cigarette papers, and all kinds of stuff. When she got caught she gave up her little book with everybody's name in it, as well as what they bought and what it was for."

"The things you see on TV about prison, most of it is an exaggeration, unless you are in there. The only thing on TV that I have seen that was remotely close was, LOCK UP. I've seen so many things in so many years".

"There was this one incident in C Cell House. It is the biggest cell house in Michigan City. A lot of times the guards don't want to walk up to the range because it is too much like work. However, when a guard did finally go up to the very top range, to the very end cell, they found a guy dead. He had been dead for about a week. If the guards would have done their job like they were supposed to, they would have found him a lot sooner, and he might have still been alive. The only way they found him when they did was because there was this real bad smell up there, and everybody was complaining about it. Only then did the guards go up and check on it."

"It was nothing to see someone committing suicide. I almost did myself, once. Five days before my execution date, I didn't want to be a circus, so I wrote a note, and put it on top of my TV, and crawled back up to my bunk, and took a razor blade, and cut the left side of my throat. My bunky,(roommate), was sleeping on the bottom bunk. I didn't think he would know anything. He woke up in the middle of the night, and when he saw all the blood, he called the guards, and they took me to hospital. I woke up in the hospital, and saw all this white hazy stuff, and I asked this lady, 'Did I make it'?' She said, 'What do you mean'? I said, 'Where am I'? I just wanted to make sure that I made it to the right place, and not the place I didn't want to go. She then told me that I was in the hospital, and they were getting ready to do surgery on my neck where I had cut through my jugular vein. After that they kept me in a coma for about a week until they started bringing me out of it. There are so many things."

"There are gangs in there that will try to come at you 5 and 6 deep to try to intimidate people. I was never much for being scared of anybody because I always think that they can't do anymore to me than I can do to them. There was this one little incident where theses little gang bangers were going to come in and take some of my stuff. They walked in talking about this is a robbery, don't make it a murder. I looked at the little bastards, and told them not to come in here, and there won't be no murder. I guess they thought they were going to try me anyway because they had their little shanks out. Then I reached under my mattress, and pulled out a sword. Man, you should have seen those guys run out. They said, 'This white boy is fucking crazy'. I told them, yeh, come back in here and see how crazy I can actually get. Needless to say, they never tried it again."

"There was so much stuff that has happened. I guess some people don't even believe that it even happens. Anything that you can get on the street, including women, you can get in there too, if you have the money."

"I do know that there was a time there on Death Row when one man was determined that he was not going to let them take him out, so he put a sheet up, which we were allowed to do for privacy. Then he tied a cord around one of the vents, and around his neck. He put a bucket on each side of him, so the blood would drain into the buckets, when he cut his wrists, so no one would see the blood, or him killing himself. When the guards took him out, they did not cover him up. They wanted to make sure everybody saw him".

"Then there was this other incident when they had had an execution. After the execution, this asshole guard came back and started talking in detail about how the

guy in the electric chair was smoking, and
described the smell in the air, and said, 'Hey
once they find you guys guilty, and send
you back here, they should put you to death
right then.' He was a captain. Some of the
guards in there are gang bangers too. They
get their records clean so that they can go in
there and take care of their little buddies—
the female guards included. In there you
have Vice Lords, Gangster Disciples, Arian
Brotherhood, Sachs and Knights, Latin
Kings, and all kinds of them, but I never
joined one. Anytime when you think you
have seen it all, you haven't even come close
because in there your worst nightmares can
come true. Believe me when I tell you that I
have seen plenty of nightmares".

Hearing some of the horrible things that Terry has lived
through, both in prison, and as a child has sent many chills up
my back to even imagine that people can be so cruel to other
human beings. If there is one lesson to be made from Terry's
story, it is to avoid prison at any cost. Some young foolish men
whom I have counseled, wear prison like a badge of courage.
Although prison is meant to teach law breakers lessons, it
teaches some people how to commit more crimes, and how not
to get caught. It also embitters some, and converts others. It
seems like a miracle that anyone can survive it, and come out
better than when they went in. I believe that Terry did do that,
at least for a little while, until he started feeling that he was
being treated differently than other people even at churches.
It was, and still is difficult for him to get jobs, even though he
has more talents and skills than most people I know.

While he was still in prison there was another group of Christians who went into the last prison where Terry was incarcerated on a fairly regular basis. They would take Christian programs into the prison, put on shows for them, as well as take food, music, and evangelists to minister to the inmates. During one of those visits, Terry was interviewed, and the interview, and his picture was published in their newsletter, and sent across this county and Canada.

I don't believe that Terry would have ever gotten out of prison if he had not been converted to Jesus Christ. The man in the original newspaper article that I read so many years ago was an angry young man, who had been wrongly accused, and saw no good people in the world since he had not seen many in his life before prison. Once in prison he saw an entire system that was corrupt, and dysfunctional. But, he had seen that before when his juvenile judge sent him back home to an abusive grandfather who had raped, beaten, and used him for target practice in the past.

Terry did not come out of prison like he was when he went in because he chose to make the best of a bad situation. The faith that he gained in prison, helped him survive 26 years of being punished for a crime that he did not commit, and the injustice system would not allow him to prove he had not committed it by allowing him to have DNA testing. I wanted to take his case to the media, but he didn't want me to because he couldn't trust the media any more than he could trust the justice system.

How many Terry's are out there now who are in danger because the child protective services are faulty, or the judicial system is blaming the innocent, and letting the real criminals do what they are best at, and go unnoticed by the law?

CONCLUSION

There is no doubt that our criminal justice system needs to be improved, even though I believe deep in my heart that sometimes God puts people in prison or gives them hardship to save their lives, or change their lives. I believe He did that for Terry. If Terry had continued to live like he had been living, he might have died before he was 30. God often allows bad things to happen to people and nations as wake-up calls for change of some sort. Perhaps that is why so many terrible things are happening in our world today. Groups like Isis are slaughtering anyone they come in contact with just for the fun of it.

Back in the Old Testament when God's people turned away from Him and started worshipping idols, and doing despicable things, like sacrificing their children, God turned His back on them, and sent other ruthless people to punish them. Jeremiah 25:15-30 is one scripture, but there are many more because the Israelites were in captivity for about 70 years in Babylon.

The stories written here are not fiction, but are real people, and stories like this continue to go on as this is being written. People are being judged by systems that are biased, and corrupt in a country that has been blessed more so than any country on earth, and innocent people are suffering for it.

If our nation is to be great, as our founding fathers intended it to be, we need to heed what the Lord said in the Bible when He was giving all the laws to Moses. God said, "Do not deny justice to your poor people in their lawsuits. Have nothing to do with a false charge, and do not put an innocent or honest person to death, for I will not acquit the guilty". (Exodus 23:6-7) Therefore, how we treat others, even as a nation, is how God will treat us. We are all responsible for what we allow in our country. I know that this book will not change the way people live, and the way that justice is administered, but there is a book that can, if people will only read it, believe it, and put it to work for them. That book is The Holy Bible. God is still in control, and if His people will repent and turn to Him, He will forgive their sins, and Bless them again.

The End

Printed in the United States
By Bookmasters